CONTENTS

W9-CIK-881

SAFETY TIPS

1. **Pay attention to all WARNINGS.** They are marked with a label like this:

Good safety practices are necessary for scientists of all ages.

2. **Wear your goggles.** They protect your eyes when mixing household or other chemicals.

3. **Don't be afraid to ask for help from adults.** Lots of adults like doing science experiments, mainly because they haven't had a chance to do any for a long time. Sometimes you may need their help, and sometimes you may want to invite adult family members to join in just for fun!

4. **Treat all substances as potentially hazardous**—for example, as flammable, corrosive, or toxic.

5. **Label all chemicals carefully, use them with adult supervision, and keep them out of the reach of young children.** Most of the chemicals in these investigations are common household substances such as vinegar, salt, and baking soda. Other chemicals are clearly marked with WARNING signs.

6. **Any time you are using the stove or matches, there is danger of fire. Make sure adults are present.**

7. **Be careful when using knives or other sharp instruments.** Wear goggles to protect your eyes.

WHAT CAN YOU DO WHEN AN EXPERIMENT "DOESN'T WORK"?

First of all, don't give up! Consider it a little challenge, and do some problem solving. Think out loud in your journal, asking yourself these questions:

1. What happened? What did you *expect* to happen?
2. Why didn't the experiment work like you thought it would?
3. What surprises did you find? What did you learn from the results?
4. What might you try differently next time? How could you test it out?

Remember: Often the most amazing and important scientific discoveries happen by accident—they are not planned. Mess around. Sometimes science is roll-up-your-sleeves, "thinking-on-your-feet" kind of work.

FORCE, OF COURSE!

FORCE & MOTION

Written by M. Leontovich

Illustrated by James Cloutier

GoodYearBooks

An Imprint of ScottForesman
A Division of HarperCollins*Publishers*

Acknowledgments
Special thanks to Mark Dow from the Willamette Science and Technology Center (WISTEC) for his insight, corrections, and enthusiasm about science . . . and for knowing (off the top of his head) the weight of a cubic foot of water; to the reference librarians at the Eugene Public Library for their tenacity and good cheer in the face of a sometimes obstructionist computerized card catalogue; to Dick Lennox, Niki Harris, Cornelia Bremer, Steven Mueller, Tamara Kidd, and Percy Franklin for their untiring spirit and hard work in getting this to disk; to Annie Vrijmoet and Nan Loveland for work on the original design and research; to Patrick Fagan for skillful and diplomatic editing on the front lines; and to the scientists, writers, and teachers in my life who explained scientific principles in ways I could understand.

GoodYearBooks

are available for most basic curriculum subjects plus many enrichment areas. For more GoodYearBooks, contact your local bookseller or educational dealer. For a complete catalog with information about other GoodYearBooks, please write:

GoodYearBooks
ScottForesman
1900 East Lake Avenue
Glenview, IL 60025

Illustrated by James Cloutier.
Copyright © 1995 Franklin & Cron Development Group, Inc.
All Rights Reserved.
Printed in the United States of America.

ISBN 0-673-36218-3 (Hardcover)

1 2 3 4 5 6 7 8 9 - DQ - 03 02 01 00 99 98 97 96 95

ISBN 0-673-36213-2 (Softcover)

1 2 3 4 5 6 7 8 9 - DR - 03 02 01 00 99 98 97 96 95

INTRODUCTION

Are you sitting down? If you're not, sit down right now. This will be your first experiment.

Sitting doesn't seem like much of an experiment, does it? But in the simple act of sitting down, all kinds of forces are at work: gravity, inertia, and friction to name a few. Even while you're reading this, forces are pushing and pulling on you and this book: air presses on you, your muscles and bones work as levers to hold the book, gravity pulls you into the chair, and friction and inertia keep you from falling off the chair. No matter what you're doing (or not doing), you're in the center of a swirl of forces that influence how you walk, talk, run, eat, and sleep.

This book is all about exploring those forces. Soon you'll start to see the forces at work all around you—the ones that enable birds to fly, apples to drop from trees, and skateboards to roll down the street. The most important thing to keep in mind while doing these experiments is that the force is *always* with you. The question is, can you find it?

CHAPTER 1
PUSHES AND PULLS

This book doesn't fall apart into a billion pieces in your hands. You're not floating near the ceiling while you read it. You'd be pretty surprised if either of those things happened, right? But books *could* fall into a billion pieces, and you *could* float. There's just one thing that's stopping you: force.

Force means anything that pushes and pulls. Force pulls your book together, and keeps you on the ground. Everything around you is pushing or pulling, and being pushed and pulled. Everything has forces acting on it all the time.

Whenever you push or pull on something, you're applying force too.

You Must Be Making This Up

Here's where it gets weird. Whenever you push on something, it pushes back. Whenever you pull on something, it pulls back. Really. So if you push on a wall, it's pushing back. And even more amazing, when you push *off* the wall, and start moving away, the wall moves away from you too. No kidding. It moves such a tiny little bit, you can't see it, but it *is* moving away. There's a special law explaining this, called Newton's Third Law of Motion. It says "For every action, there is an equal and opposite reaction." The "action" in this case was you moving away from the wall. The "opposite reaction" is the wall moving away from you.

Here's an easier example. Have you ever tried to throw a ball while you're on a swing? Try it sometime (but be careful). When you throw the ball forward, you go *backward* in the swing. The *action* (throwing the ball) produces an opposite *reaction* (you go backward). In the next few experiments we'll look at a few other examples so you can see it happening.

JUMP UP!
When you jump up, as you move away from the Earth, the Earth is moving away from you too! It's true. But it moves so little you can't measure it.

HMMM... I WONDER ...IF EVERYONE IN CHINA JUMPED AT EXACTLY THE SAME TIME, WOULD IT PUSH THE EARTH OUT OF ITS ORBIT...?!?

EXPERIMENT 1: IT WORKS IN WATER

This experiment will use water to demonstrate Newton's Third Law.

1. Use the nail to punch two holes in the rim of the cup. Make sure the holes are exactly opposite each other.

Now thread the string through the holes and tie the two ends together to make a loop. This loop is your handle.

2. Fill the cup with water and hang it over the sink. Is it hanging straight down? If it's tilted in one direction or another, your holes need to be fixed. Try again until the cup is hanging straight down.

3. Empty the cup of water. Now punch three or four holes in the side of the cup, near the bottom. Make all the holes close together on one side.

4. Put the cup over the sink again and quickly fill it with water. The water should start streaming out of the bottom, moving away from the cup. That's an action. Where's the reaction? (**Hint:** What position is the cup in now?)

SUPPLIES
tall paper or plastic cup
nail
string
water

FIRST THINGS FIRST!
Newton also had a First Law of Motion, which says that an object that's standing still won't ever move unless something pushes or pulls on it. It also says a moving object will keep moving until something pushes or pulls on it to make it stop. Look around you for examples of moving objects. What makes them move? What causes them to stop?

MY MOM HAS A FIRST LAW OF MOTION, TOO... IT SAYS, "IF I DON'T GET OUT OF BED THE FIRST TIME SHE CALLS, I CAN FORGET HAVING BREAFAST!"

INVESTIGATE SOME MORE!
If you have a small hose attachment on your sink, or a hose outside, try this: Turn on the water, holding the hose in one hand, and let the water pour out against your other hand. Do you feel a push on your hand in the water? What about the hand that's holding the hose? Where does the hose go when you let go?

SUPPLIES

balloon
several yards of string
drinking straw
masking tape
clip to hold the balloon
    closed (optional)

EXPERIMENT 2: BLAST OFF!

If you've ever blown up balloons, you've probably seen Newton's Third Law in action. This experiment shows you how it works.

1. Tie one end of your string to a solid object like a tree (if you're outside) or a door handle (if you're inside). Thread the other end of the string through the straw.

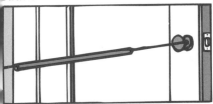

Now tie the other end of the string to something else (a chair is good), pulling the string tight so it makes a straight line.

2. Blow up the balloon and tape it to the straw. Make sure you don't let any air out of the balloon while you're taping it! And don't let the tape touch the string, just the straw.

3. Drag your straw and balloon all the way over to one end of the string. Now let go of your balloon. What happens? Since you know every action has an equal and opposite reaction, can you name the action? the reaction? (**Hint:** What you *saw* was the reaction. Can you figure out what was moving in the opposite direction?)

4. Set up a duplicate experiment using another balloon, another string, and another straw right next to the first one. Have balloon races with a friend! This is not particularly scientific, but it's fun. Maybe you can explain Newton's Third Law while you're racing.

INVESTIGATE SOME MORE!

Keep an eye on things that are moving. Can you spot the *action* and *reaction* in every movement? In your science journal, draw pictures of each motion, showing where you think the action and reaction are.

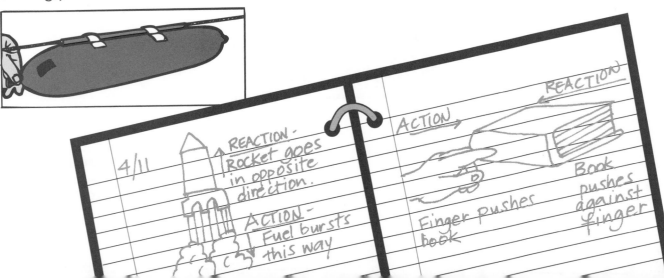

EXPLORE SOME MORE

ANCHORS AWAY!

Even though you know every action has an equal and opposite reaction, some are pretty hard to see (like the Earth moving away when you jump, for example). This one is easy. For this experiment you will need 2 milk or juice cartons, 2 pencils or dowels, tape, rubber bands, and scissors.

1. Tape shut the carton so no water will leak in. This is the body of your paddle boat.

2. Attach two pencils on either side of your boat using pencils or dowels. Make sure the pencils go 5 or 6 inches past the bottom of the boat.

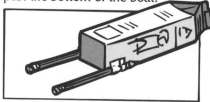

3. Cut out two squares from your other carton. Make the squares an inch smaller than one side of your boat. (For example, if your boat is 4 inches across, make the squares 3 inches). Cut a slit *halfway* down each square. Connect the squares at the slits as shown.

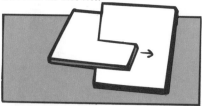

This is your paddle.

4. Loop your rubber band over the back ends of the pencils. Make sure the rubber band is stretched flat. If it isn't, the rubber band is too big, so try a smaller one. Now slip the paddle between the rubber bands so it is held in place.

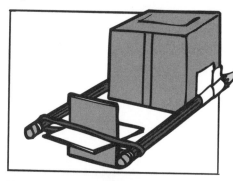

5. Turn the paddles with your finger so the rubber band twists. Place the boat in the water and let go. What happens? Watch the water. What direction is the water going in? What direction is the boat going in? Can you see the action and reaction? Does this prove Newton's Third Law?

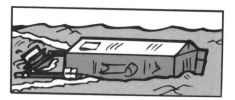

WHAT IF?

Imagine you are an astronaut, floating in space outside your capsule. Suddenly, the line tying you to the capsule breaks and you start floating off into space. All you have to save you is the screwdriver you were using. How are you going to get back to the capsule? How can Newton's Law help?

AW, SHUCKS

Scientists measure everything, even how much force is needed to move, speed up, or slow down an object. They measure this in units called "newtons," in honor of Sir Isaac Newton.

> SO HOW MANY NEWTONS WILL I NEED TO STRIKE OUT THIS NEXT BATTER..?

FOR FURTHER EXPLORATION
The Forces With You! by Tom Johnston (Milwaukee, WI: Gareth Stevens, 1988).

STOP RIGHT THERE

Watch something move, like this book, for example. Take a second to put this book down on a table, then give it a small push. (Go ahead, I'll wait.) So what happened? The book moved when you applied force. It's also interesting to note that the book eventually *stopped*.

Scientists not only wonder why and how things move, they wonder why things *stop* moving. Why didn't the book just keep going? Some force must have been working on the book to make it slow down and finally stop.

Making and Breaking Bonds

That force is **friction.** Friction happens when two surfaces (like the book and the table) come in contact with each other. Both the book and the table are made of tiny molecules. When two objects are together, some of the molecules in one object link up with the molecules in the other. When you pushed the book, you forced these links (or bonds) apart.

Then more linked up and were forced apart again as the book kept moving. This constant linking and breaking of the bonds causes heat. If you've ever rubbed your hands together, you've felt this heat yourself.

Our whole lives depend on friction. Without friction this book would slip out of your hands no matter how tightly you tried to hold it. Without friction the floor would be more slippery than ice. Food would slip off your fork which you wouldn't have been able to hold in the first place. This book would still be moving across the table after you pushed it, although it would have been difficult to push in the first place (too slippery!). Let's hear it for friction!

OLD SMOOTHIES

There's friction even in water. Whales and dolphins have extremely smooth skin that lets them move through water with very little friction. Their skin is so smooth that scientists are studying it. They'd like to make a skin equally smooth for boats and submarines. So far, no luck!

BALD IS BETTER

Why do you think many competitive swimmers, both male and female, shave their bodies?

SURVIVAL SKILL

You know that people used to rub two sticks together to start fires. The fire starts because of the heat caused by the friction.

Read more about friction and kinetic energy in Chapter 5 of *Power Up!*

EXPERIMENT 1: THERE'S THE RUB

What affects how much friction there is? This experiment will help you find out.

1. Cut a piece of string about two feet long. Tie the ends to one end of the rubber band. Make a red dot with your marker where they meet. Now take a two-inch piece of string, and tie one end to the *other* end of the rubber band.

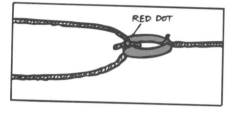

RED DOT

2. Draw a straight line down the middle of your piece of paper. Tape the short piece of string to the top of the paper, right on top of the line.

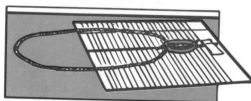

3. Lay the string and rubber band along the line. Make a mark where the rubber band and long string meet (right at the red dot), and write "0" above it. Write a number for every ruled line going down the page, starting with "1." This will be your *line scale* for measuring friction.

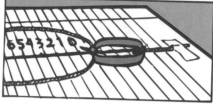

4. Lay a book flat on the table and loop the long string around it. Keep the paper flat and grab the taped short string. Pull away from the book, making sure the loop and rubber band stay over the line scale.

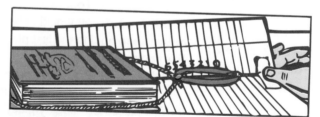

Watch where the red dot is on your scale, and mark where it is as the book starts to move. Keep pulling the book. Where is the dot along the scale now? Did it change?

5. Do the experiment again with the book balanced on its edge so less of it is touching the table. Where on the scale is the dot when the book starts moving? Did it take more force to pull the book or less? Does that mean there was less or more friction?

6. Do the experiment a third time with two books on top of each other. Mark the place where the red dot is when the book starts moving. Is there more or less friction now? Does weight make a difference?

INVESTIGATE SOME MORE!

Do the experiment with other objects and on other surfaces (the carpet, the sidewalk, whatever surface you see). Use both light and heavy objects, and smooth and rough surfaces. In your journal, keep track of which objects and surfaces create the least and most friction. Does weight make a difference? What about the size of the surfaces that touch? What about the smoothness of the surface?

EXPERIMENT 2: OUTFOXING FRICTION

Although friction is handy to have around, sometimes you don't want a lot of friction. What can you do to lessen friction?

1. Do Experiment 1 again. Mark on your line scale the position of the red dot when the book starts moving.

2. Line up the straws or pencils under the book.

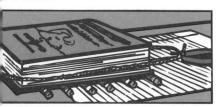

Place the book on top. Now pull on your scale and mark where the red dot is this time when the book starts moving. Is there more or less friction? Which surfaces are touching? Are they rolling or rubbing, or both? Which creates less friction?

3. Now put the book on the table. Place your hand on top of it and try to spin it. What happens? Now put the plastic lid on the table, and place the marbles in it. These marbles are like the ball bearings used in machines.

4. Place the book on top. Put your hand on top of the book and try to spin it again. What happens this time? Is it harder or easier to spin?

In your journal, write down what you've learned about friction. Does weight make a difference? the amount of places the objects are touching? Why is it easier to move something using wheels?

GULP!
Have you ever tried to swallow food that's really dry? It's hard to do! Your body fights this friction by making lots of saliva to help the food slide down.

PUTTING ON THE BRAKES
It's a good thing that friction slows things down. Take a good look at the brakes on your bike to see how they work. When you use your brakes, a piece of rubber or plastic presses against the rim of your wheels. The friction between the rubber and the rim stops your bike.

INVESTIGATE SOME MORE!
Look around you for objects with wheels. How are the wheels used to fight friction? If the wheels couldn't turn, what would happen? Is there anything that could be used in place of wheels?

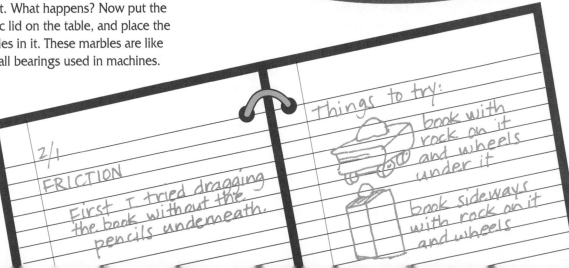

EXPLORE SOME MORE

SLIP SLIDING AWAY

In the introduction to this chapter you read that without friction you wouldn't be able to hold anything. One way you can test for friction is by seeing how easy something is to hold. In this experiment you'll learn now to reduce friction by using different **lubricants.** Lubricants reduce friction by preventing the surface molecules from rubbing together. This experiment is messy, so do it in the kitchen, and put down plenty of newspapers. Try doing this experiment with a friend, taking turns to see who can transfer the most cubes in the least amount of time.

For these experiments you'll need: 5 envelopes of unflavored gelatin, water, 2 large mixing bowls, vegetable oil, liquid dish detergent, measuring cup, butter knife, newspapers, clock or watch with a second hand, square baking pan, your line scale, a heavy book, and a plastic bag (large enough for the book).

WARNING ! DO NOT EAT THESE CUBES! THEY DON'T TASTE VERY GOOD WHEN THEY'RE PLAIN, AND YOU CAN GET SICK IF YOU EAT THEM WITH DETERGENT ON THEM.

1. In a bowl, mix the five packets of gelatin into 2-1/2 cups of hot tap water. Rub a little vegetable oil on the insides of the baking pan, then pour in the gelatin mixture. Refrigerate until firm (about 4 hours).

2. Use your butter knife to cut the gelatin into 1-inch squares. Put 10 of them into a bowl.

3. Place the second bowl one or two feet away. Take squares out of the first bowl one at a time and place them in the second bowl. See how many squares you can transfer in ten seconds. Then have your friend try it. Make a chart in your journal to keep track of how many you can transfer each time with a different lubricant.

4. Now return the squares to the first bowl, and pour some detergent on them. Make sure they're coated. Now see how many you can transfer to the second bowl in ten seconds. Could you transfer more or less? Do you think there was more or less friction? Have your friend try it. Did your friend get the same result? Record your times on your chart.

5. Discard those cubes. Using new cubes each time, do the experiment several more times using different lubricants. Try covering the cubes with water. Try oil. Which ones were the hardest to hold onto? Which ones were the easiest? Which substance was the best lubricant? the worst? Write down the results in your journal.

LET'S DO IT AGAIN

Ask permission before you do this experiment, since it can be messy.

1. Try your book experiment again. This time, tightly wrap a heavy book in a plastic bag and tie a knot at the top. Place the book in a shallow baking pan, and do Experiment 2 with your line scale, marking the spot on the scale showing where the book starts to move.

2. Now coat the bottom of the baking pan with oil. Place your book in the pan. What happens when you try to pull the book now? Which was more effective—lubrication or the pencil wheels from Experiment 2? What would happen if you tried both, and lubricated your wheels?

LOOKS LIKE RYAN IS DOING HIS FRICTION EXPERIMENT AGAIN!

CHAPTER 3
WHAT GOES UP....

What goes up must come down. Everybody knows that, right? If you hold this book over the floor and let go, it goes *down*.

But what about astronauts in space? If you've seen videos of them in their space capsule, you know everything in the capsule floats—the astronauts, their books, their tools, *everything*. They even eat things out of tubes and straws so their food doesn't get away from them. Why does this happen? Why doesn't everything work the same way as it does here on Earth?

A Matter of Matter

First you have to know about **matter.** Matter is anything that has mass and takes up space. (**Mass** is another good word to know. Something has mass if you need to push on it to make it move.) Everything you see is matter. Even something you can't see, like a tiny molecule, is matter, since it takes up space (not much, but some) and has mass. A molecule is matter. You have mass and take up space, so you're matter too. So is this book.

All matter pulls on all other matter. This pull is called a **gravitational pull.** The more matter, the bigger the pull. This book is pulling on you right now, but it's too small a pull for you to notice it. The Earth, however, has *a lot* more matter than the book, so it pulls hard. When you held out your hand to drop the book, the Earth pulled the book toward it. So the next time you hear someone say "What goes up must come down," let them know they really should be saying "What goes up, must go *toward*"—toward the Earth in this case.

SPACE WALK
Why *do* you think astronauts in space can float?

THE MAN WHO GREW TOO MUCH
Astronauts "grow" two or more inches while in space. Their spines stretch out when they're weightless, giving them extra height. When they get back to Earth, they shrink back to their usual size again. One very tall astronaut on the space shuttle grew too much—in space he was taller than the maximum height allowed for astronauts!

EXPERIMENT 1: COME SWING WITH ME!

In this experiment you'll see how gravity affects pendulums (PEN joo lums). You'll start by watching gravity pull objects toward the center of the Earth.

1. Tie your washer (or clay) to the end of the string.

2. Fix the other end of the string to the edge of a table using the piece of tape.

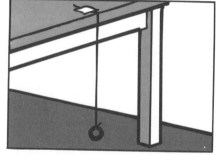

Wait a minute until the washer and string are motionless. Where is the washer pointing? Where do you think the center of the Earth is?

3. Now for your pendulum: Place the book upright on the ground a foot or so away from where the washer is dangling. Now lift the washer until it's right against the book, and let go.

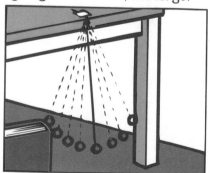

4. Watch the pendulum swing. Does it hit the book on its next swing? How far away from the book is it on each swing? What happens after a minute or two? If you know that gravity is pulling the pendulum toward the Earth, how does that affect the swing of the pendulum?

5. Now make another pendulum using your other washer, this time making sure the string is *shorter* than the last one. Tape this one to the edge of the table. Do the experiment again, starting *both* pendulums from the edge of the book. Watch their swings. Do they reach the end of their swing at the same time? Is one faster? slower? Why do you think this is? How long does it take each pendulum to come to a complete stop?

In your journal, write down the results of your experiment. Explain any differences you found. How can the Earth's gravitational pull explain what happened? Do you think you could draw a diagram of how the Earth pulls on your pendulums?

IT MUST BE HERE SOMEWHERE

Knowing about gravity helps astronomers find planets. Astronomers noticed that Uranus' orbit around the sun was slower than they thought it should be. They decided something big, like a planet, must be pulling on it to slow it down. By watching Uranus' orbit they figured out exactly where this new planet must be, and then looked into the sky. There it was—Neptune!

INVESTIGATE SOME MORE!

Try again using two strings of the same length, but with one washer on one string, and two or three washers on the other string. What happens when you let them go at the same time and from the same spot? Are their swings the same speed? How long does it take each one to come to a complete stop? What effect does weight have?

SUPPLIES
bean seeds
plastic sandwich bag
a few paper towels
brown paper bag
water

11

EXPERIMENT 2: GROWING DOWN

All life on Earth grows with gravity pulling on it. In fact, we've learned to depend on it. The experiment below shows one way living things depend on gravity.

1. Fold over a few paper towels until they're the size of the plastic bag. Wet them down so they're moist, but not dripping. Put them into the plastic sandwich bag.

2. Place six or seven bean seeds in the bag against the wet paper towel. Press them against the side so they don't move around, or all land at the bottom.

3. Stand the bag with the seeds upright, opening to the top, inside the paper bag (seeds don't like light).

BODY BUILDING
Your body depends on gravity just like plants do. When astronauts are weightless for a long time, their bones start to weaken, and their heart rate slows down. Why do you think this might happen?

Check on them every few days to see if roots start to grow, and add a little water if the paper towels start to dry out. Every time you put the plastic sandwich bag away, remember to stand it upright with the opening toward the top.

4. In a few days you should see roots forming. In your journal, draw pictures of the beans and roots. In which direction are the roots growing? Are they fighting gravity? After the roots have been growing for a week or so, place the plastic bag into the paper bag upside-down. Leave it for a few days. Can you *predict* what will happen, and why?

5. Take out the plastic bag and look at the roots. Now which direction are the roots growing? Draw the seeds and roots in your journal. Why do you think roots need to know which way is down? What would happen if they didn't? How does gravity help plants grow?

REAL BOTTOMLESS PITS
Some collapsed stars have very strong gravitational pulls. Their pull is so strong that nothing can escape them, not even light! Scientists call these stars **black holes.** Anything that gets too near a black hole will be sucked in.

INVESTIGATE SOME MORE!
Put one or two of your seeds in a small pot and let them grow until they have 4-6 leaves. Then turn the pot on its side and leave it for a few days or a week. What happens? What do you think would happen to a plant if you grew it in space where there's little or no gravitational pull?

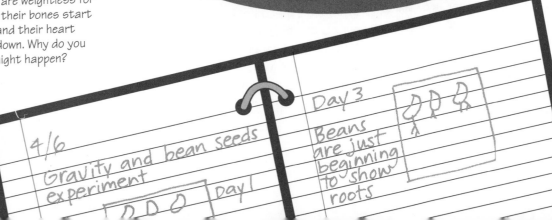

EXPLORE SOME MORE

ANOTHER PIECE OF PISA

You've probably heard about the Leaning Tower of Pisa. It's famous, not only because it's leaning, but because of a story people tell about a man named Galileo, who lived over 400 years ago. Back then there were two ideas about gravity's effect on falling objects. Most people agreed with Aristotle (who had lived even longer ago), who said that heavier objects fall faster than light ones. Galileo thought all objects, light and heavy, fell at the same speed. One day, the story goes, Galileo decided to test his idea. He climbed to the top of the Tower of Pisa with a light wooden ball and a heavy metal ball, and dropped them over the side to see which hit the ground first.

Oh well. It's a great story, and Galileo *did* drop two objects, but he didn't drop them from the Tower of Pisa. He dropped them from two **inclined planes** (inclined planes look like wedges). You can be Galileo and try the experiment. Like Galileo, it won't involve the Leaning Tower, but it does make a good story.

Note: You can use any two objects that are about the same size and shape, but which have very different weights. Try a rock and a Ping-Pong ball, or a grape and a marble or ball bearing. Make sure they won't break if you drop them!

1. Check to make sure the two objects you're using have very different weights. If you have a scale, you can weigh them. Sometimes just picking them up can tell you one is heavier than the other.

2. Stand on a chair. Hold out the two objects at the same height. What do you think will happen? Will one object hit the ground first? Why or why not? Let them go at exactly the same time. What happened? Who was right, Aristotle or Galileo? What did you learn about the pull of gravity on falling objects? Write down your results and ideas in your journal.

3. Do the experiment again using objects of different shapes, like a ball and a piece of paper. Is there a force other than gravity at work here? In your journal, write down your ideas about what happened.

THE TEN MINUTE MILE

Think of your favorite sport. How would it change if the Earth's gravity

were stronger or weaker? For example, if you picked track, would your running times be faster or slower? Would you change the height of the hurdles? What about the pole vault?

Pick your favorite sport and redesign it for a planet with more gravity, and for one with less gravity. Do you think you'd like the sport better on another planet? Why or why not?

CARRY THAT WEIGHT

Imagine you're on a planet with a much stronger gravitational pull. In your journal, write down what would be hard for you to do. Could you walk? run? eat? Could birds fly? Could cats leap? Could plants grow? Write down how your body would have to change to work well on the planet. Now design an alien creature that would be well suited to such a place. How would it be different from creatures on Earth, and why?

Imagine your body on a planet with a much weaker gravitational pull than that of Earth. How would your body change this time? What would an alien who lived there look like? Draw your ideas in your journal.

FOR FURTHER EXPLORATION
The Science Book of Gravity by Neil Ardley (London: Dorling Kindersley, 1992).

A BALANCING ACT

Have you ever watched babies learn how to walk? They fall down a lot. When you were little you fell down too. Now that you're older, you're much better at staying upright. Think about a time recently when you almost fell over. Your arms pinwheeled and your heart raced until you got your balance back. You could probably *feel* the exact moment when you knew you weren't going to fall.

You've been learning about gravity. Unlike babies, you're good at making sure you don't fall over when you walk or run. You have a sense of balance. But what is balance? And why do you <u>lose</u> your balance?

What's the Point?
Something is balanced when all the forces pushing and pulling on it cause it to stay still. You can see this if you pick up a spoon. Put one finger under the spoon until it's balanced.

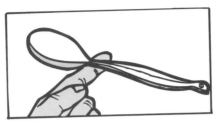

When the spoon is still and is not wavering at all, it's balanced, or at **equilibrium.** What you've found is the balancing point, or **center of gravity** for the spoon, the one place where all the gravitational forces pulling on it make it balance. The place where your finger is under the spoon is the **support point.** This is the rule for balancing things: An object balances whenever the support point (your finger) is directly under, over, or on the object's center of gravity.

Now put something heavy on one end of the spoon, like a coin or a small rock, and try to balance the spoon again. Is your finger in the same place it was last time? Where is the center of gravity for the spoon now? Why? Now that you know about equilibrium and centers of gravity, can you guess why you fall over sometimes? What is your body good at finding that babies aren't?

Your center of gravity is somewhere below your stomach and above your hips.

IN THE CENTER RING
High-wire performers in the circus usually carry a long pole while they walk across the wire. Try walking in a straight line while holding a pole or broomstick. How does it affect your center of gravity?

I DON'T THINK THAT'S THE WAY YOU'RE SUPPOSED TO CARRY IT!

EXPERIMENT 1: BIZARRE BALANCES

SUPPLIES
pencil
three forks
quarter
lump of clay or a potato
string
drinking glass
book
toothpick
rubber bands

You can just look at some objects and guess where the center of gravity is. Others are not so easy. In this experiment you'll create bizarre contraptions and then try to balance them! For each figure, answer the following in your journal:

> Where is the center of gravity?
> Where is the support point? Is it *above, below,* or *on* the center of gravity?

1. Stick the tines of two forks into a lump of clay or small piece of potato. Stick a toothpick halfway into the clay. Now try to balance this contraption on the edge of the glass, as shown. Does it balance? Where is the support point? the center of gravity? Now point the forks in the other direction. What happens?

2. Cut out a slice of potato, and stick a pencil through the middle. Stick a fork into the side of the potato slice. Can you balance this on the edge of a book?

3. Using two forks, a potato, and a pencil, create the contraption shown.

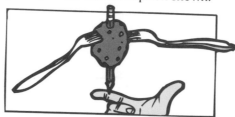

4. Wrap the rubber bands around the forks as shown. Attach a piece of clay or potato to the end of one of the forks with another rubber band. Can you balance this on the edge of a table?

A QUESTION OF BALANCE
Why does changing the placement of objects change the center of gravity? Do you think everything has a center of gravity? Can everything be balanced? Why or why not?

I WONDER
Will things balance in outer space? Is gravity important to make things balance? Why or why not?

INVESTIGATE SOME MORE!
Using the potato, forks, pencil, and toothpick, create as many of your own contraptions as you can. Try to find each one's center of gravity. In your journal, draw each contraption and show where you think the support point and center of gravity is. Try giving the contraptions to friends to see if they can balance them.

EXPERIMENT 2: LIFE IN THE BALANCE

Objects aren't the only things that balance. Since you're not falling over all day, you must be balancing too. Can you find your own center of gravity? Does it change? Why or why not? Try the experiments below. For each one, see if you can figure out:

- Where your center of gravity is
- When or how it moves, if at all
- Where your point of support is
- When you can feel yourself losing equilibrium

1. Stand against a wall with your left foot, your left shoulder, and your left cheek pressed to the wall. Now lift your right foot. What happens? Why? How can you change the experiment to alter your center of gravity and change the result?

2. Sit in a straight-backed chair with your feet flat on the floor. Keep your back against the back of the chair. Now fold your arms over your chest. Keeping your back straight against the chair, stand up. What happens? Now get up out of the chair the way you usually do, *but do it in slow motion*, and watch where your body goes. What's different this time? Is it important for your body to be able to find the center of gravity? Why or why not?

3. Stand with your heels against a wall. Now bend over and touch the floor. What happens? Can you feel when your center of gravity shifts?

OUCH!

What would happen if your body could not adjust the position of your center of gravity? How would your world be different?

TALL TAILS

Cats and squirrels change the position of their tails to change their center of gravity. That's one of the reasons they have such great balance.

IT'S ALL IN THE TAIL..!

THAT'S EASY FOR YOU TO SAY!

INVESTIGATE SOME MORE!

Do the same experiments again and see what happens:
—when you keep your eyes closed
—when you carry something heavy in one hand or the other
— when you have an adult man try them
—when you have an adult woman try them
Is there any difference in what happens?
—even a slight one? Can you guess why?

EXPLORE SOME MORE

STUCK INSIDE A MOBILE

Mobiles are a form of moving art. Artists who build mobiles intentionally use pieces with different shapes, sizes, and weights. Materials with different centers of gravity help make the mobile look and move in interesting ways. Use what you've learned about centers of gravity to make your own mobile.

For this experiment you'll need string, cardboard, construction paper, pens, markers and/or crayons, glue, drinking straws or dowels, stiff wire and nails or pushpins, glitter, paint, and stickers (optional).

1. Cut out 6 to 10 different shapes and sizes of cardboard (depending on how big you want your mobile to be). Decorate each side of each shape using construction paper, pens, markers, glitter— whatever you want! You might want to have a theme for your mobile. For example, each piece might represent a member of your family, a friend, an endangered species, or a tesselation (see *On the Move!*, Chapter 10).

2. Tie a length of string around the middle of a straw or dowel.

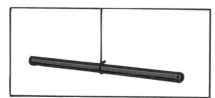

(You may have to use glue to keep the string in one position, or you can punch a small hole through the straw and thread the string through this.) This is the first piece of your mobile.

3. Punch a small hole in the top of your pieces of cardboard using a nail or pushpin. Thread pieces of string through the holes, making a loop, and tie the ends together. Start hanging these pieces from the ends of the other straws or dowels. Try hanging one an inch or two closer to the middle. What happens?

Experiment by making longer and shorter strings, hanging different size shapes on each end, and by changing where on the straw or dowel you hang the pieces. Then check for balance by balancing the straw on your finger.

4. Now it's time to put all the pieces together.

You may have to adjust which pieces go where, depending on the weight and center of gravity of each piece, or you might move or lengthen the strings that attach them. When you're done, hang the mobile in your room and watch it sway and move in the air currents. Can you see why artists who make mobiles have to know a great deal about gravity?

FOR FURTHER EXPLORATION
Why Doesn't the Earth Fall Up? by Vicki Cobb (New York: Dutton, 1988).

CHAPTER 5
THAT SINKING FEELING

Have you ever dropped a penny into a fountain? It sinks right to the bottom. Pennies are too heavy to float, right? But wait a minute, you're much heavier than a penny, and *you* can float. A giant cruise ship is very heavy, but it can float. Why?

Believe it or not, gravity makes some things float and some things sink. As an expert on gravity, you know it's pulling everything toward the center of the Earth, including water, and anything you put on (or in) the water.

A Weighty Matter

Water is heavy (you know if you've ever tried to carry a bucket of water). Water has a lot of mass, and gravity pulls hard on it. How much water weighs makes all the difference in floating. Imagine you have a box that is one cubic foot (that means a foot on each side). One cubic foot of water weighs about 62 pounds. If your cubic foot box weighs *less* than a cubic foot of water, gravity will pull down less hard on your box than on water, and your box will float. If your box weighs *more* than 62 pounds, gravity will pull down harder on your box than on the water, and your box will sink. So to decide if something will float, just imagine it's made of water. Ask yourself, Would this be heavier if it were made of water, or would it be lighter? Even though a cruise ship is big and made from heavy steel, it has

a lot of empty space. An amount of water as big as the cruise ship would weigh much, much more. So, the ship floats.

There's a special name for all this: **buoyancy.** That's the force that pushes up on anything lighter than water. It also pushes up on things that are heavier than water, but not enough to stop them from sinking. That's why things seem to weigh less in water. Did you ever try to pick up a friend in a swimming pool? It's easy! Buoyancy is helping you pick them up.

CAN'T BE DONE?
Everyone laughed at the engineers who first tried to make a boat out of steel. Up until then, boats were made of wood, which is very light. Everyone thought a heavy steel boat would sink. The engineers who made it understood the principle of buoyancy and successfully launched the first steel boat in 1823.

For more about the energy of water power, see *Power Up!*, Chapter 7.

EXPERIMENT 1: SHIPSHAPE

SUPPLIES
large glass or small basin
water
clay
small scale (optional)
plastic bag (optional)

Is weight the only thing that affects buoyancy? In this experiment you'll see if shape has anything to do with whether things float or not.

1. If you have a small scale, start by weighing the clay. Now form the clay into a ball about the size of a plum, and drop it in the glass of water. What happens? What do you think is heavier, the piece of clay or a blob of water the same size as your piece of clay? How do you know?

2. Now take your clay ball and make it look like a fat thimble.

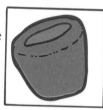

Drop it in the water. What happens? Which weighs more—the clay thimble or an amount of water the same size as the clay thimble?

3. Now take your thimble and make it into a small fat cup that's slightly larger than the thimble.

Drop it in the water. What happens? Which weighs more—the clay cup or a blob of water the same size as the clay cup? How do you know?

4. Use the same piece of clay and make larger shaped things with it by making the clay thinner and thinner. Make your last shape a large boat. As you finish, drop each shape into the water. In your journal, describe what happens as your shapes get larger. Which sizes and shapes sink? Which ones float? What happens if your shape fills with water?

5. If you have a scale, weigh your clay boat. Does it weigh the same as the ball did at the beginning? Now fill your boat to the top with water. Pour this water into a plastic bag, knot it, and place it on the scale. Which weighs more, a boat-sized amount of water or the boat? You can see why people make boats with lots of empty spaces in them. In the next experiment, you'll learn more about the effect of size and shape on the ability to float.

DON'T CROSS THIS LINE!
Any boat will sink if it carries too much cargo. That's why all boats have a line called a **Plimsoll line** drawn on the side. When water hits the line, it means the load is too heavy and the boat might sink. Where's the Plimsoll line on your clay boat?

TIPPING THE SCALES
A ship's size is measured by its **displacement.** Displacement is the amount of water that's pushed aside when the ship is put in the water. The weight of the displaced water is the same as the ship's weight!

INVESTIGATE SOME MORE!
Drop other objects in your glass of water (chunks of different vegetables work well). Make a chart in your journal to keep track of which ones weigh more than the same amount of water, and which weigh less. Can you explain why?

EXPERIMENT 2: PUSHUPS

SUPPLIES

pencil
string
scissors
2 glasses
2 weights of the same size (washers will work great)
water
tape
table or chair

Buoyancy pushes up on things. In this experiment you'll look at how that affects weight.

1. Cut two pieces of string about 8 inches long. Tie one washer to the end of each string. Now tie the other ends of the string to each end of a pencil.

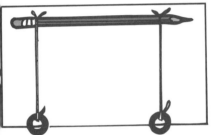

2. Take the rest of your string and tie one end to the middle of the pencil. Tape the other end to the edge of the chair (ask permission first!), making sure your washers hang a few inches off the floor.

Make sure the middle string is in the direct center of gravity on the pencil, and the washers are balanced.

3. Put each glass under a washer, so the washers each hang inside the glass. Are they balanced? Do they weigh the same? Now fill one of the glasses with water while the washer is still in it. What happens? What effect does the force of buoyancy have?

INVESTIGATE SOME MORE!

Look around for a heavy object. Now decide you're going to move it using water to help you. In your journal, design a way you can move the object using water. Explain why you think it will work.

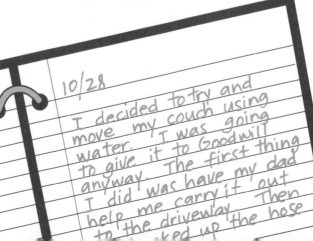

10/28

I decided to try and move my couch using water. I was going to give it to Goodwill anyway. The first thing I did was have my dad help me carry it out to the driveway. Then ... ked up the hose

EXPLORE SOME MORE

THE PLOT THICKENS

What happens when you try to float water on water? You'll need 3 balloons, 3 fairly large jars or containers, and water for this experiment.

1. Fill a jar with water and put it in the refrigerator until it's very cold. Fill the second jar with very warm water from the tap. Fill your third jar with water and leave it at room temperature.

2. Fill your 3 balloons with equal amounts of room-temperature water. Knot each balloon.

3. Take your cold water out of the refrigerator. Place one balloon in the cold water, one in the room-temperature jar, and one in the jar of warm water. What happens?

Knowing what you know about weight, gravity, and water, is some water heavier than others? lighter? Did temperature make a difference? Write in your journal what happened, and make some guesses about temperature's effect on water.

SAIL AWAY

You know shape is important for floating. Try designing some different shapes for boats and see which one holds the most weight.

You'll need 6 sheets of aluminum foil, a tub or sink, and pennies for this experiment.

1. Cut all the foil sheets so they're the same size. Now start building a boat by folding the foil into different shapes. Make sure you build one boat:

- with a flat bottom (like a raft)
- with a deep bottom (like a cup)

Otherwise, experiment wildly. How about a square boat? a pyramid-shaped boat? a canoe?

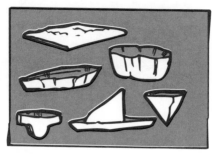

2. Once you've built 6 different boats, float them on the water. Do they all float? If not, can you figure out why?

Now start putting pennies into your boats. Make a chart in your journal to keep track of which boat holds the most pennies before sinking. Which boat holds the fewest pennies? Which shape is best for keeping large weights afloat? Discuss the results of your boat test in your journal. Explain why you think each boat held the number of pennies it did.

3. Boat builders not only think about weight, they also think about how a boat moves through the water. Blow on your boats to create a wind, or make a sail of a Popsicle™ stick, a sheet of paper, and a lump of clay. Test each boat. Does it move quickly through the water? What design is best for going fast? Can that design be made to hold weight too? Which design is hard to steer? easy to steer? Next time you're out near a lake, river, or ocean, look at the boats there. What do their designs tell you?

NOT EXACTLY BUILT FOR SPEED IS IT...?

FOR FURTHER EXPLORATION
Scientists by Struan Reid and Patricia Fara (London: Usborne, 1992).
Boat by Eric Kentley (New York: Alfred Knopf, 1992).

CHAPTER 6
FORCES IN A WET WORLD

Think about raindrops. You've seen them a million times. You've also seen the round beads of water that fall on the kitchen counter when you spill something. Why are there rain*drops?* Why not rain*cubes* or rain*pyramids?* Why aren't there little *star*-shaped blobs on your counter?

All Together Now
Water molecules like to stick together. This is called **cohesion.** And the best shape for staying together is a round ball or sphere. This way no molecules are sticking out (which would happen in the points of a star or pyramid shape).

Because of cohesion, water can do something else—it gets a kind of skin on top. A skin can form because of the way water molecules like to stick together. In a glass, or on a pond, all the water molecules pull on each other in all directions, except for the ones on the surface. There are no more water molecules above them to stick to, just air! Since water molecules are not as attracted to air—they'd much rather stick to each other—It takes some work to break apart these water molecules on the surface. This is called **surface tension.**

IT'S ART, NOT SCIENCE
Raindrops are always drawn with a point at the top, but the fact is, raindrops don't have pointy tops. They flatten out like a squished ball because of the force of the air they're moving through.

WALKING ON WATER
Have you ever seen a bug walking on the top of a lake or stream? These are called water striders, and they actually walk on top of the water, using surface tension to hold them up.

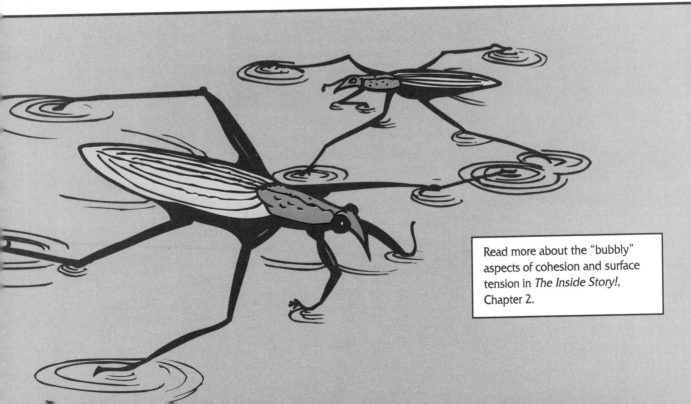

Read more about the "bubbly" aspects of cohesion and surface tension in *The Inside Story!*, Chapter 2.

EXPERIMENT 1: LET'S STICK TOGETHER

SUPPLIES
eyedropper or straw
glass
water
bowl
paper cups
coin
tack or nail

This experiment is actually a game you can play with a friend. Take turns adding water. Try not to be the one who makes it spill over!

1. Fill your glass exactly to the rim with water. Now carefully place it in a sink (the water will spill later).

2. Fill your bowl with water and put it near the glass.

3. Fill the eyedropper or straw with water from the bowl. Take turns with your friend adding ONE DROP of water to the glass each turn. Watch the water carefully. What's holding it together? How many drops can it hold? What shape is the water? Can you guess why? Keep adding drops until the water spills over.

You can do the same game with a coin. Drop water, one drop at a time, on top of a coin. What shape is the water's surface? Keep doing this until the water runs off the coin.

The Same Only Different

1. Punch three small holes close together on one side near the bottom of a paper cup.

2. Stand over a sink and add water to the cup. The water should be streaming out of the three holes.

3. Now use your fingers to pinch the streams of water together. Take your fingers away. What happens? How does this affect the stream? Why?

4. Do the cup experiment again, making the holes closer than the last time. This time, don't use your fingers to pinch them. How close does water have to be to stick together? Now, using a new cup, make the holes farther apart. Does it still work? How far apart do the holes have to be before water stops sticking together?

INVESTIGATE SOME MORE!

Try this experiment using other liquids: milk, juice, vinegar, oil, and so on. How does it change with each kind of liquid?

3/1 Glass filled with water   with oil   with milk

Keesha and I tried this with water first. We added 15 drops, then when Keesha added the 16th ...

EXPERIMENT 2: SKIMMING ALONG

SUPPLIES

bowl
water
paper clips
tape
construction paper
pens, crayons
scissors
sink or tub

After you see surface tension in action, you can make racers that will glide on the surface of water. Hold your own races with your friends!

1. Fill the bowl with water. Bend one part of the paper clip so it points straight up and makes a handle. (Keep in mind that not all paper clips are made the same way. Some float and some don't. Try different kinds until you find one that does.)

2. Carefully place the flat part of the paper clip on top of the water. Let go. What happens? Look carefully at the water around the paper clip. Is the clip in the water or on top of the water? Is it breaking the surface? How is standing on the surface different than floating?

3. Use your construction paper to cut out small figures of people small enough to stand on a paper clip! Leave a tab of extra paper at their feet.

You'll use this to attach them to the paper clip. Draw in faces and give each one its own special racing colors.

4. Make a small loop of tape, sticky side out. Attach this to the top of a paper clip. Now fold over the tab on the feet of one of your racers and press this onto the tape. Do this for all of your racers.

5. Gently place your racers on top of the water in the sink or tub, and gently blow on them (be careful not to blow them over!). The first one to reach the other side wins!

What do surface tension and bubbles have in common? See *The Inside Story!*, Chapter 2.

THE QUICKER PICKER UPPER

Lots of paper towel companies say their paper towel is more absorbent than others. Are they saying water is more "attracted to" their towel? Test this by placing drops of water on different brands of paper towels. How does the water act each time? Is it more attracted to one kind than another? Do you think some are more attracted to water? Why or why not?

INVESTIGATE SOME MORE!

Once you have a paper clip on top of the water, add a small drop of detergent or liquid soap. What happens? In your journal, discuss what you think is happening in the water. What do you think happened to the bonds between the molecules of water? Did the soap make them stronger or weaker? Try adding small amounts of other liquids to the water. What happens to the bonds each time?

EXPLORE SOME MORE

ABSORBED IN YOUR WORK

Water not only likes to stick together, it can also form bonds with other things. This is called **adhesion** (ad HEE zhun). The molecules in water bond well with some things and not so well with others.

Put drops of water on the following objects and watch what happens. How can you tell when the water would rather just stick to itself? How can you tell when it likes to stick to something else?

Place a drop of water on these man-made objects:
- different types of paper
- a raincoat
- waxed paper
- aluminum foil
- cotton T-shirt
- polyester T-shirt
- a countertop
- a magazine cover
- a glass
- something painted
- waxed furniture

Which objects attract water? Which objects seem to repel water? In each case, why is it a good idea that each thing attracts or repels water? Does it make it more or less useful to people and under what conditions? Do you think designers keep this in mind when they make things? How do you know?

Now place a drop of water on some natural things:
- your skin
- a leaf
- soil
- rocks
- fur

Do each of these things attract or repel water? In your journal, discuss what would happen if each thing acted in the opposite way. How would the world be different if something that usually repels water suddenly started attracting water, or vice versa?

CREATIVE COHESION

You can use the cohesion of water to make a game that uses drops of water as the game pieces! You'll need waxed paper or aluminum foil, water, a pencil, and a friend for this experiment.

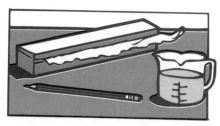

1. Cut a sheet of waxed paper or foil about 16 inches long. Now draw a simple maze on the surface with your pencil. This will be the race course for your water drop, so don't make it too complicated. Start simple at first.

2. Use a pencil to poke three holes somewhere along the route of the maze. These will be "traps" for your drop.

3. To play, place one drop of water at the starting gate. Now, holding the paper in your hands, tilt it to start the water drop moving through the maze. If you go outside the lines, go back to that point and start over. Be careful to avoid the traps!

4. Time yourself to see how long it takes. Now have a friend try it and see if he or she can do it faster.

5. Try drawing different mazes. Make them more complicated, or add more traps. Then try making the maze out of different kinds of paper. Which ones make it easier? harder?

FOR FURTHER EXPLORATION
Science for You—112 Illustrated Experiments by Bob Brown (Blue Ridge Summit, PA: Tab Books, 1988).

LIGHTER THAN AIR?

Who says air is light? Well, maybe it's lighter than a bowling ball or a rock. But air does weigh something.

The Earth is surrounded by a blanket of air. (By the way, can you guess what holds it in place?) The blanket is miles high, so there is a lot of air above you, pushing down. This force is called **air pressure.**

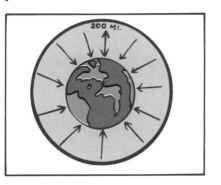

Don't Weigh Me Down

Look at your arm. Now imagine a one-inch-square box drawn on your skin. Scientists figure that air pushes on you with a weight of 15 pounds on that square inch. Imagine how many boxes like that could fit on your body.

EITHER THESE SCALES ARE BROKEN OR THE AIR IN THIS ROOM IS HEAVIER THAN USUAL!

That adds up to a lot of heavy air! The good news is the pressure of the liquid inside our bodies pushes out at the same time the air pressure is pushing in. If it didn't, we could be crushed by something as light as air!

Although air pressure always pushes on us, it's not always exactly the same. When air gets warm, the molecules tend to spread out. When it gets cooler, the molecules are closer together. Do you think one kind of air might push harder? In the next few experiments we'll look at air and find out.

IF ONLY YOU HAD A SCALE...
The air in a large room can weigh as much as a full-grown adult!

DEEP BREATHING
We depend on air pressure to breathe. When we inhale air, a muscle called the *diaphragm* pulls down, making more room in our lungs. With all this extra room, the air pressure in our lungs is now lower than the air pressure outside. The outside air pushes its way into our lungs.

You can find out more about air in motion in *Power Up!*, Chapter 6.

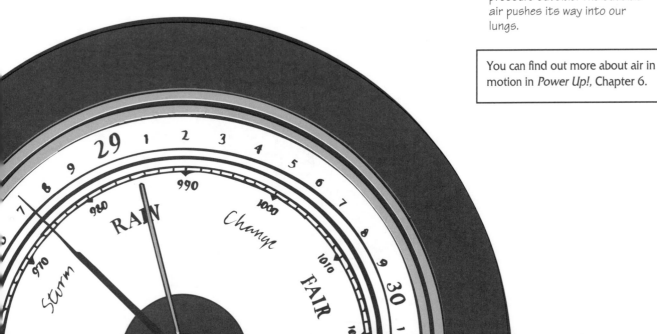

EXPERIMENT 1: AIR POWER

SUPPLIES

jar
funnel
water
clay
balloon
heavy book

It's easy to take air for granted. As these two experiments will show, air has a lot more force than you think.

1. Place your funnel in the jar and seal the place between the funnel and the jar with clay. Make sure there are no holes for air to escape.

2. Slowly pour water into the top of the funnel. What happens?

3. Make a hole in the clay. What happens? What do you think is happening in the jar?

More Air Power

1. Put a book on the edge of a table. Place the body of the balloon under the book. Keep the open end of the balloon peeking out over the edge of the table.

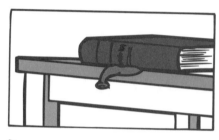

2. Try to blow up the balloon. What happens?

AIR POWER VERSUS HORSE POWER

Air wants to rush into places where there is no air. In 1654 a German scientist named Otto von Guernicke took two halves of a hollow metal ball, put them together, and pumped all the air out. The outside air pressure pushed the two halves together, trying to get inside the ball. It pushed so hard that two teams of horses couldn't pull the two halves apart!

WHATEVER IS INSIDE THAT BALL MUST BE VERY IMPORTANT!

INVESTIGATE SOME MORE!

Drop a balloon into a jar, leaving the end outside the jar. Lean over the jar and blow up the balloon. What happens? What do you think causes it? In your journal, write down what happens, and draw pictures of the experiment. Show where the force of air pressure is in this experiment by including arrows in your drawing.

SUPPLIES

clear plastic soda bottle
with screw-on cap
refrigerator

27

EXPERIMENT 2: A SLIGHT CRUSH

If warm air has a different pressure than cold air, what happens when you put the two together? In this experiment you'll find out.

1. Leave your bottle in a place where it can get nice and warm, outside in the sunshine, or in a sunny window.

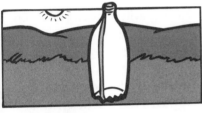

WARNING BE CAREFUL NOT TO PUT IT NEAR SOMETHING HOT—PLASTIC CAN MELT!

2. Once your bottle is warm, put the cap on. Then put it someplace cold—outside if it's winter, or in your freezer.

3. Watch the bottle. What happens? Can you see air pressure working on the bottle?

4. Unscrew the cap. What happens? What do you hear or feel as you loosen the cap?

In your journal, draw a diagram of the bottle during all phases of the experiment. Draw arrows showing where you think the air is pressing at each stage. Explain your reasoning.

AIR SHARE

We tend to think of air and oxygen as the same thing, but it isn't. Actually, only about 20% of air is oxygen. Most of the rest is nitrogen. Believe it or not, breathing pure oxygen is bad for you!

DID YOU KNOW SCOTTISH PHYSICIAN DANIEL RUTHERFORD DISCOVERED NITROGEN IN THE AIR IN 1772?

WEATHER REPORT

You know that air pressure changes with temperature. The pressure of air can tell you a lot about the weather. Check the weather map in your newspaper every day for a week. Does it show high or low pressure in your area? Is the weather sunny or rainy? Keep a chart in your science journal showing the pressure and the weather for each day. What kind of weather do you get when there's high pressure? low pressure? Does this help you predict the weather?

INVESTIGATE SOME MORE!

Air molecules get farther and farther apart as you go up in the atmosphere. If you fill a bottle with air at sea level and then hike up a mountain, what do you think will happen when you open the bottle? Try it!

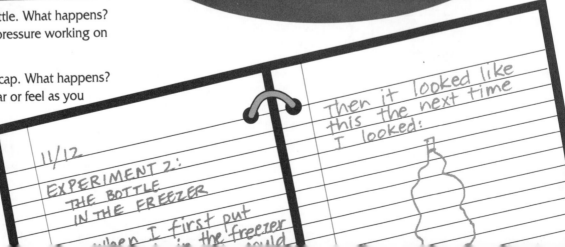

11/12

EXPERIMENT 2:
THE BOTTLE
IN THE FREEZER

when I first put
in the freezer

Then it looked like
this the next time
I looked:

EXPLORE SOME MORE

WIND+WATER+GRAVITY=ART

Now that you're an expert on these three things, it's time to put all this knowledge to some creative use. Make some art using water, colors, and your own breath! Even gravity will help you! For this experiment you will need different kinds of white paper, food coloring or water, paints, water, a drinking straw, good lungs, newspapers, and small bowls or glasses.

1. Begin by placing newspapers down where you're going to work. This can get messy!

2. Put a piece of white paper down. Now put equal amounts of water and *one* food color in one of the bowls. Use your other bowls or glasses to mix other colors with water. These will be your paints.

3. Use your straw to put a drop of one of your paints on the paper. Use your straw to blow hard on the drop until the color skitters across the paper. Try it again using another color.

4. Lift your arm high and let drops of color fall on your paper. What happens? What happens when the drop falls from farther away? Does it look different? How is gravity affecting your art?

5. Try other kinds of paper. Try one that water is very attracted to. Try one that water doesn't like as well. How does this change your art? (Now you can see why painters are choosy about what paper they use.) Add some water to your paper to make it damp, or to swirl the drops together. Use your imagination!

Let your artwork dry, and then hang it where everyone can see it. Remember, you needed both art and science to make this work of art.

If you have a chance, look up the work of an artist named Jackson Pollock (the library will have books on him). Take a look at his paintings. What forces do you see at work?

NOTHING UP MY SLEEVE

Use air pressure to do a magic trick. This can be pretty messy too, so work over a sink the first time you try this. For this experiment, you will need a glass, water, and a piece of cardboard.

1. Fill your glass to the very top with water. Cut out a square of cardboard that will cover the top of the glass.

2. Slide the cardboard over the top of the glass. Make sure the cardboard is touching all parts of the rim! You don't want to leave any holes or gaps for air or water to move through.

3. Put one hand under the glass and one hand on top of the cardboard. Quickly turn the whole thing upside down.

4. Remove your hand from the cardboard on the bottom. What happens?

You know gravity is pulling down on the water in the glass and on the cardboard. You also know there is air pressure all around. So who's winning? Why? Try the experiment again with a glass half full of water. What happens this time? In your journal, write your ideas about this. Once you get really good at doing this trick, show it to a friend.

FOOD FOR THOUGHT
Would this be a good magic trick if everyone knew a lot about air pressure? How much do tricks rely on people not knowing things?

MY OWN PERSONAL OPINION IS —THE DUMBER THE AUDIENCE, THE BETTER THE MAGICIAN!

FOR FURTHER EXPLORATION
Physical Forces (Alexandria, VA: Time-Life Books, 1992).

CHAPTER 8
FLIGHTS OF FANCY

Have you ever watched a big passenger plane take off? It doesn't seem possible that something that large can get off the ground. But it does, by riding on air. You know air has weight and pressure. But how can it hold up a whole plane?

It manages, thanks to a force called **lift.** Lift is air pressure that pushes up on things. Air pressure isn't always the same, though—it changes with speed. The faster air moves, the less the air pressure it has.

Think about an airplane wing, or a bird's wing (see *The Inside Story!*, Chapter 8). It's curved on top.

The curve makes air molecules speed up and spread out, going faster over the wing than under the wing. The faster moving air on top has less pressure, so the slower air underneath pushes *up*, creating lift.

Onward and Upward
You have to move fast to get enough lift to get off the ground. Planes move forward to make air rush over their wings. This forward force is called **thrust.** That's why airports have long runways; planes have to get up to a good speed before the lift is strong enough to propel them off the ground.

There are two forces working against planes: **gravity** and **drag.** As you know, gravity wants to pull everything toward the Earth. Drag is the word for friction caused by air. Molecules of air rushing against the plane slow it down. That's why birds and planes are shaped the way they are—their narrow, smooth design causes less friction. What do you think would happen if someone tried to build a plane shaped like a cube?

OLD-FASHIONED IDEAS
A scientist named Daniel Bernoulli discovered that the faster liquids and gases moved, the less pressure they had. This is exactly what happens with the air going over an airplane's wing. This idea is called **Bernoulli's principle,** and he figured it out over 200 years ago!

ANOTHER WAY TO FLY
Another way to fly is to make your plane lighter than air! Anything that weighs less than air will float in air, in the same way objects lighter than water will float in water (remember Chapter 5?). Blimps and some balloons are filled with helium (HEE Lee um), a gas that weighs less than air. That's how they float!

EXPERIMENT 1: MOVE ASIDE

SUPPLIES
two balloons
string
a straw
scissors
tape
piece of paper
blow dryer

Bernoulli said that air moving quickly has less pressure than air moving slowly. Here are three ways to see Bernoulli's principle in action. Before you start, write down what you think will happen in each experiment. Were you right? Were there any surprises?

1. Blow up the balloons so they're about the same size, and knot them. Cut two pieces of string and tie these to the ends of the balloons. Use tape to hang the balloons from a doorway, making sure they hang at head level, with about 8–10 inches between the balloons.

2. With your straw, blow air between the two balloons. What happens? Do they move farther apart or closer together? Where is the air moving fast? slow? Where does the air have low pressure? high pressure? Does this agree with Bernoulli's principle?

Even Easier

1. Hold a piece of paper to your face, right below your bottom lip.

Blow straight across the paper. What happens? Does it push the paper down or up? Why?

2. Use a blow dryer on the "cool" setting and blow across the top of the paper. What happens?

Now set the dryer on "hot" and try the experiment again. What happens this time? Does temperature make a difference? Why or why not?

In your journal, sketch both experiments, showing where the air is moving. Draw arrows to show where air pressure is pushing on the paper and on the balloons. Where's the lift?

INVESTIGATE SOME MORE!

The next time there's a windy day, take a look at all the things that are lifted off the ground. In your journal, draw their shapes. Take some guesses at their weight too. What do these things have in common? Were you surprised to see that some objects didn't lift up? Why do you suppose they didn't?

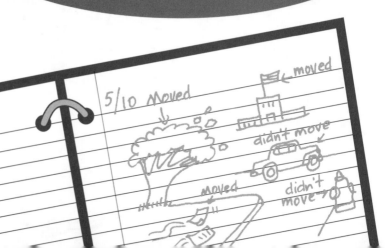

EXPERIMENT 2: IT'S A DRAG

Drag isn't always a bad thing. Sometimes we depend on drag. Take parachutes, for example. Try making the parachute below and see if you can spot what creates the most drag.

1. Cut an 18-inch circle out of a plastic garbage bag.

2. Cut 6 pieces of string, each about 12 inches long. Tape one end of each piece of string to the edge of the circle. Tie the other ends into a knot.

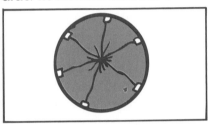

3. Wrap a ball of clay around the end of the strings, or tie them to a small action figure or toy.

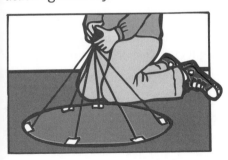

4. Throw your parachute into the air. What happens? What pulls the toy down? What keeps it up? Where is the air friction?

5. Make a few new parachutes—a square one, and a rectangular one. What happens?

6. Make a bigger parachute, then a smaller one. Which one works best? Why? Which one increases drag?

FALLING FREE
Before they open their parachutes, skydivers fall through the air at about 118 miles per hour!

I'M GOING TO HAVE TO CITE YOU FOR SPEEDING!

SUPPLIES
string
tape
scissors
plastic garbage bag
piece of clay (or a small action figure)

HOT STUFF
You know friction causes heat. Even friction from air can make things hot. When a meteor or a space capsule enters the Earth's atmosphere, the friction caused by moving through the air can make them so hot they burn up! That's why space capsules are made from special materials that won't burn— even at high temperatures.

I'VE EATEN A COUPLE OF TACOS THAT TASTED SO HOT, THEY MUST HAVE COME FROM OUTER SPACE.!!

INVESTIGATE SOME MORE!

Use a smaller ball of clay, or lighter action figure; then use a bigger one, and then use none at all. How does each change affect the parachute? Make a sketch of your different parachutes in your journal and explain why you think some worked better than others.

EXPLORE SOME MORE

FLOATING ON AIR

Use these illustrations and directions to make a paper airplane.

1. Fold an 8-1/2 x 11" sheet of paper in half.

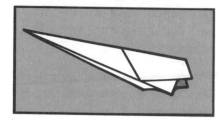

2. Fold the two top corners toward the center crease.

3. Fold each side again toward the center crease.

4. Turn the sheet over. Now fold each side to the center crease.

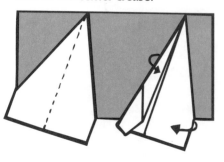

5. Fold paper along the center crease.

6. Now open out your plane. The plane may fly better if you tape it on the spots shown in the illustration.

If your plane doesn't fly as well as you'd like, make some adjustments. Try attaching a paper clip to the nose, or to the middle of the plane.

You may also create tail flaps to alter direction.

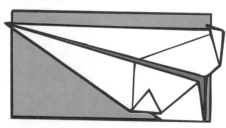

Why do you think each of these things changes how the plane flies?

BIRDS DO IT

For centuries, people have been trying to fly. They've created all kinds of winged contraptions for getting a person off the ground. Unfortunately, most didn't know about Bernoulli's principle, or lift.

You do. Knowing what you know, design and draw a one-person flying machine. In your plans, be sure to include:

- How your wing design will give you lift
- What you will use to get enough thrust
- How you'll overcome the fact that a person is pretty heavy
- How it will be powered (by pedaling? flapping your arms?)
- How it will be shaped to lessen drag

You may not be able to build it, but test out your ideas on paper. You might even try building a small model of your final design. Bon voyage!

TOPSY-TURVY
Aerobatic planes have wings that create lift even when they're upside-down!

FOR FURTHER EXPLORATION

Airborne, The Search for the Secret of Flight by Richard Maurer (New York: Simon & Schuster, 1990).

A Bird's Body by Joanna Cole (New York: Morrow, 1982).

WHAT'S THE ATTRACTION?

There may be some magnets on your refrigerator right now. You've probably had magnets as toys. They're fun to play with, and they're handy for holding things on the refrigerator. But what are they? How do they work?

The force that makes magnets work is called—what else?—**magnetism.** It's a force that pulls on some materials. To learn why some things are magnets, you have to know about atoms.

Tiny Tugs

Atoms are the tiniest particles that make up all things. Atoms have a tiny magnetic pull. They also spin a little, like a top. In most things, the atoms are spinning every which way, pulling on each other in all directions.

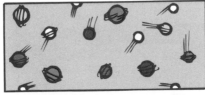

In a magnet, the atoms start to line up.

Now all their little pulls are added together to make one big pull. Think about a tug of war you've seen, with two teams of people pulling against each other on a rope. If everyone is pulling on the rope in a different direction, no one goes anywhere. If they all start pulling in the same direction, they can really pull hard! This is what happens in a magnet.

You know magnets won't pick up some objects. Did you ever wonder why? When a magnet does pick up an object, the atoms in that object start lining up. The object becomes a magnet too! But only while it's near the first magnet. Once you move it away, its atoms spin all over the place again. There are lots of objects whose atoms just won't line up at all (like you, for instance). These are the objects magnets can't pick up.

WHAT'S IN A NAME?
A long time ago, people found rocks that iron would stick to. They found these rocks in a place called Magnesia, so they called the rocks "magnes." That's how magnets got their name.

THESE IRON ORE ROCKS WERE ALSO KNOWN AS "LODESTONE."

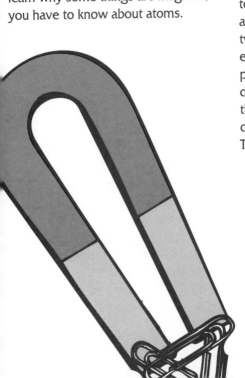

EXPERIMENT 1: OUT IN THE FIELD

SUPPLIES
steel wool
goggles
gloves
2 magnets
a piece of paper
scissors
pin

WARNING ! STEEL WOOL CAN CAUSE SPLINTERS. WEAR GLOVES AND GLASSES DURING THIS EXPERIMENT, OR HAVE AN ADULT HELP WITH THE STEEL WOOL.

The **magnetic field** is the direction and amount of force that can be felt near a magnet. This experiment helps you see the direction of the magnetic field around the magnet. While you do this experiment, keep in mind that this is only *part* of the magnetic field: the field keeps on going and going and going.

1. Wearing gloves and glasses, use scissors to cut up the steel wool into little pieces, or have an adult help you with this.

2. Lay the magnet down and cover it with the piece of paper. Gently tap some of the steel wool out onto the paper over the magnet.

3. Gently tap the paper. What happens to the steel wool? What kind of patterns are produced?

4. Try bringing a pin toward the magnet. When do you feel the pull? Is the pull inside or outside the magnetic field?

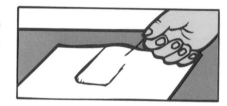

5. Try the experiment again, using the two magnets, with opposite poles an inch or two apart. Place the paper over both, and sprinkle the steel wool. Tap gently. What happens this time?

6. Try the experiment with like poles together. How does this affect the magnetic field? What looks different? What effect, if any, are they having on each other?

POLES APART
Every magnet has two poles—a north pole and a south pole. These opposite poles are attracted to each other. If you put two like poles together, they push apart!

INVESTIGATE SOME MORE!

In your journal, draw the outline of the part of the magnetic field you saw. (You didn't see all of it, remember? It keeps on going!) Now place the magnet on the paper and attach a paper clip to the magnet. Keep attaching paper clips to each other until they will no longer hold together. What happens? Mark where the clips stop attaching. What does this point represent?

iron nail
strong bar magnet (a
  refrigerator magnet is
  probably too weak)
paper clip

EXPERIMENT 2: UP AND ATOMS

Can you make atoms line up just right? In this experiment you'll see if you can cause the atoms in a nail to line up and become magnetized.

1. Touch your nail to the paper clip. Do they attract? Is either of them a magnet? Are the atoms all pulling in the same direction?

2. Very slowly stroke the nail with your magnet. ALWAYS STROKE IN THE SAME DIRECTION! ALWAYS STROKE THE NAIL WITH THE SAME PART OF THE MAGNET. (That's why you're using a bar magnet: It's hard to use the same spot on a round magnet.)

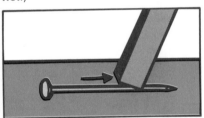

After 5 strokes, touch it to the paper clip again. What happens? Do you think the atoms are pulling in the same direction now?

3. Keep stroking the nail with your magnet. After every 5 strokes, test to see if it has become magnetized by touching the paper clip. Do this until you've done 50 strokes.

4. In your journal, write what happens each time you test the paper clip. When does the clip become magnetized? Does it get stronger with more strokes? Is there a point where more strokes don't make a difference? Why? In your journal, explain what you think is happening.

5. Use your magnet to stroke your clip in all different directions. Rub it backwards with the magnet, stroke it in different directions, or touch it with different parts of your magnet. After every 3 strokes, test your nail by trying to pick up the other paper clip again. What happens?

INVESTIGATE SOME MORE!

Do the experiment again. This time, once your nail has become magnetized, drop it on the floor. Now test it on the paper clip. Keep dropping the nail and testing it on the clip. What happens? Can you guess why? What are the atoms doing? What force is working on them?

10/2

EXPERIMENT 2:
MAKING MAGNETS

After 5 strokes, I
tried touching the nail.
I felt a small pull
this time! So I
stroked the nail against
the magnet another 5 times

EXPLORE SOME MORE

NORTH AND SOUTH

The biggest magnet on Earth is the Earth itself! Like all magnets, it has its own magnetic field. This field is pulling on your small magnet. Within the Earth's field, a magnet will line up going north and south. Unfortunately, the Earth's magnetic pull isn't as strong as two other forces working on your magnet—gravity and friction.

As you know, there's one substance that can both make something weigh less and reduce friction—water! If you float a very light magnet on water, you can see the Earth's gravitational pull in action. There's a special name for a magnet that is free to line up this way—a compass! A compass points north and south because the giant magnet Earth is pulling it that way. In this experiment you'll be making your own compass. See for youself! You'll need a bowl (not a metal bowl!), water, needle, piece of cork or Styrofoam™, paper clip, and a store-bought compass for this experiment.

1. Magnetize your needle just the way you did in Experiment 2. Make sure it's magnetized by testing to see if it attracts a paper clip.

2. Stick the needle through a small piece of cork or Styrofoam™. Float this in a bowl of water. What happens? Compare it with your store-bought compass. Which end of the needle is pointing north?

3. Gently move the needle with your finger and then let go. What happens? What happens if you jiggle and turn the bowl? Can you fool the Earth's magnetic field?

TREASURE HUNT

Compasses don't just show you the Earth's magnetic field at work. They're also used for giving directions. Have a treasure hunt with your friends, and use a compass and map to help them find the treasure.

1. Decide what your "treasure" will be, and hide it before your friends come.

2. Pick an exact spot where they will start their search. Now use your compass and write down directions on how to find the treasure. For example, you might write "Take two steps due south. Then take four steps to the southeast...."

3. Before they start, have each of your friends make their own compass using the directions above. Also give them a picture of the points of the compass so they know exactly where each direction is.

4. Give them your instructions and see if they can find your treasure using a map and compass. Since your compass is in water, they may have to stop each time to let the water settle to take a reading. Make sure it doesn't all spill out!

ARE WE ALMOST THERE?
People have been using compasses to find their way for over 900 years. But they didn't know about the Earth's magnetic field, so they didn't know why a compass worked. That made it hard to trust the magnet's direction!

WHERE'S THE MAP?
Some birds migrate over long distances every year. Scientists think some kinds of birds find their way by sensing where they are in the Earth's magnetic field.

FOR FURTHER EXPLORATION
Physics for Kids—49 Easy Experiments with Electricity and Magnetism by Robert Wood (New York: McGraw Hill, 1990).
KnowHow Book of Experiments with Batteries and Magnets (New York: Sterling, 1976).

CHAPTER 10
GO TO WORK!

You're doing work all the time, even if you don't have a job. Picking up this book took work. Turning the pages takes work. Any time you apply force to something, you are doing work. How much work it is depends on how much force you have to use. Picking up this book didn't take much force at all. Picking up a boulder (if you could do it) takes a lot more force, and is more work.

Force isn't the only thing that affects the amount of work needed to complete a task—so does distance. Bringing this book across the room is work.

Bringing it ten miles is a lot farther, and a lot more work. When you measure how much work you're doing, you have to measure both the force and the distance.

Handy Helpers
Nobody wants to work harder than is necessary. If you look around you right now, you can probably see several machines that help us do work more easily. The machines you're looking at are probably pretty complicated.

There are some machines, called **simple machines,** that help us do work too. They either let us use less force, or cover less distance. The complicated machines you're looking at have simple machines inside them. Even your body uses simple machines! In this chapter we'll see how simple machines make work easier.

PULL YOURSELF UP
In your body, muscles do most of the work. Muscles never push on your bones to get you moving, though. They can only pull. Whenever you start moving, a muscle somewhere is pulling on your bones. Move your arm or leg. Which muscle is pulling? Now move your arm or leg in the opposite direction. Which muscle is pulling now?

EXPERIMENT 1: LOVE A LEVER!

SUPPLIES
heavy book (a dictionary
would be great!)
1 or 2 foot board
fat marker (your ful-
crum)

One kind of simple machine is called a **lever.** A lever is just a bar and a pivot (called a **fulcrum).** If you've ever pried open a can of paint with a screw-driver, you've used a lever!

There are different kinds of levers, but they all have a bar and a fulcrum. They also have a **load,** which is the force of the thing you're trying to move, and a place where force is applied (in this case, that just means where you push or pull on the bar).

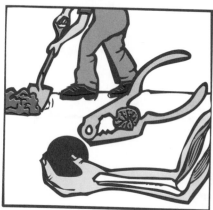

In this experiment, you'll be lifting a book using different levers.

Try out all the different arrangements of load (book), fulcrum, and bar pictured below. Keep track of where you apply the force. Does that make a difference? Which lever makes it easier to lift the dictionary? Which one makes it harder?

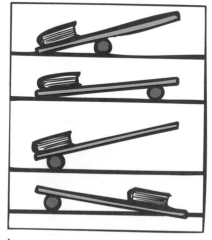

In your journal, keep track of how well each lever worked. If you had to move a boulder, where would you place the fulcrum? Where would you apply the force? Why?

GOLDEN OLDIE

Over 2,000 years ago, a Greek scientist named Archimedes (ark a MEE dees) figured out how and why levers worked. People had been using levers for a long time, but he was the first to explain them using math. He's famous for saying "With a big enough lever, you can move the world." Do you think this is true?

INVESTIGATE SOME MORE!

Try all the levers again using a smaller fulcrum, and then try a larger one. Try a longer and a shorter board. Do these changes make a difference in how easily you can lift the dictionary? How?

SUPPLIES
wooden board two or
three feet long
two heavy books

EXPERIMENT 2: IT'S PLANE TO SEE

Another simple machine is called an **inclined plane.** If you've ever seen a ramp, you've been looking at an inclined plane. In this experiment, you'll try to push a heavy book up an inclined plane to a certain spot. Experiment with the different kinds of inclined planes shown below. In your journal, describe which one makes it easiest to move the load. Which one makes it hardest?

1. Try all the inclined planes below. Use one book to support the board, and push the other book up the plane.

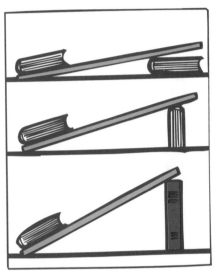

2. For each plane, measure and record in your journal the distance between the beginning of the ramp and the place where your book "support" starts. Was it easier to push the book when the distance was shorter or longer? If you needed to move something very heavy, which design would you use? Why?

BACK AND FORTH
On mountains or steep hills, roads and walking trails don't go straight up the mountain—it would be too difficult to walk or drive that way. Instead, the road winds back and forth up the mountain. These inclined planes are called **switchbacks,** which are easier to climb.

OLD NEWS
The pyramids in Egypt are made of huge stone blocks. For years people have been wondering how they moved all those heavy blocks around. The best guess is the Egyptians pushed the blocks up inclined planes in order to build the pyramids.

INVESTIGATE SOME MORE!

What forces were working against you when you pushed the book up the inclined planes? In your journal, write your ideas on making it even easier to push the book uphill. What forces could you overcome? How? Explain why you think it would work.

EXPLORE SOME MORE

FIND THE FORCES

Look at the drawing below. All the forces you learned about are working in the picture. Take a good look and see if you can answer the following questions. Record the answers in your journal. Be sure to give good reasons for your answers.

- Where do you see an example of buoyancy?
- Can you see places where friction is helping them eat and drink? Is anything being lifted? Is there something shaped like a lever involved? (**Hint:** Look for something shaped like a bar that has a support point or fulcrum.)

- Can you find an example of cohesion?
- Can you find an example of Bernoulli's principle?
- What in the picture is resisting gravity?
- Do you see any examples of thrust?
- Can you find an example of lift?
- What simple machines are in the picture?
- Is there anything or anyone in the picture whose support point is not under, over, or on their center of gravity?
- How many examples of Newton's Third Law of Motion can you find? Name the action and reaction.

- Are there places in the picture where the air pressure is weaker than in others? Where? How do you know?
- Can you find a friction-fighter in the picture?
- Is there anything in the picture that's lubricated? (**Hint:** look for something that might be hard to pick up with your fingers.)

WHEELS AT WORK

Wheels are a kind of simple machine. Look around your environment for wheels. How do they help you do work? Do you need less force to do something if wheels are involved? Why or why not?

FOR FURTHER EXPLORATION

Janice VanCleave's Machines by Janice VanCleave (New York: Wiley, 1993). *Machines and How They Work* (New York: Dorling Kindersley, 1991).

adhesion when the molecules of two separate things want to stick together

air pressure the force of air pushing on things

Bernoulli, Daniel a scientist who discovered that the faster a liquid or gas moves, the less pressure it has

Bernoulli's principle a theory that says the faster a liquid or gas moves, the less pressure it has

black holes places in space where stars have collapsed, causing a gravitational pull so strong that even light can't escape

buoyancy the force in liquids and air that pushes up on things

center of gravity where weight is centered in an object

cohesion occurs when molecules are attracted to each other and stick together

compass a tool showing the direction of the Earth's magnetic field

displacement the amount of water pushed out of the way when an object is placed in the water

drag friction caused by air on moving objects

equilibrium occurs when all the forces pushing on an object cancel each other out, causing the object to stay still

force anything that pushes or pulls on an object

friction the process that occurs when two objects move against each other, causing them to make and break molecular bonds

fulcrum the support piece beneath a lever

gravitational pull the pull of an object on other objects; the more mass an object has, the stronger its gravitational pull

gravity the force in every object that pulls on other objects

inclined plane a simple machine, shaped like a wedge, that makes it easier to move an object

lever a simple machine that uses a bar and a fulcrum to make it easier to lift loads

lift occurs when air pressure forces objects to rise

load the weight or mass you are trying to move with a lever

lubricant any substance that reduces friction

magnet any object that has a magnetic pull

magnetic field the area around a magnet that still has a magnetic pull

mass the amount of matter in something; a large, heavy object has more mass than a small, light one

matter the substance of an object; anything that takes up space

newton a unit for measuring force

Newton's First Law of Motion a law stating that objects that aren't moving won't move unless something pushes or pulls on them; and that moving objects will keep moving until something pushes or pulls on them to make them stop

Newton's Third Law of Motion a law stating that whenever a force pushes or pulls, another force will push or pull in the opposite direction

pendulum an object that is free to swing back and forth under the influence of gravity

Plimsoll line a line painted on a boat to show how much cargo it can carry without sinking

simple machines basic machines used to make work easier such as the wheel and axle, pulley, inclined plane, lever, wedge, and screw

support point the place that holds up an object; if the support point is over, under, or on the center of gravity, the object will balance

surface tension the attraction between molecules that causes a "skin" of strong bonds to form on the surface of water

thrust the forward motion of planes, jets, and other flying machines